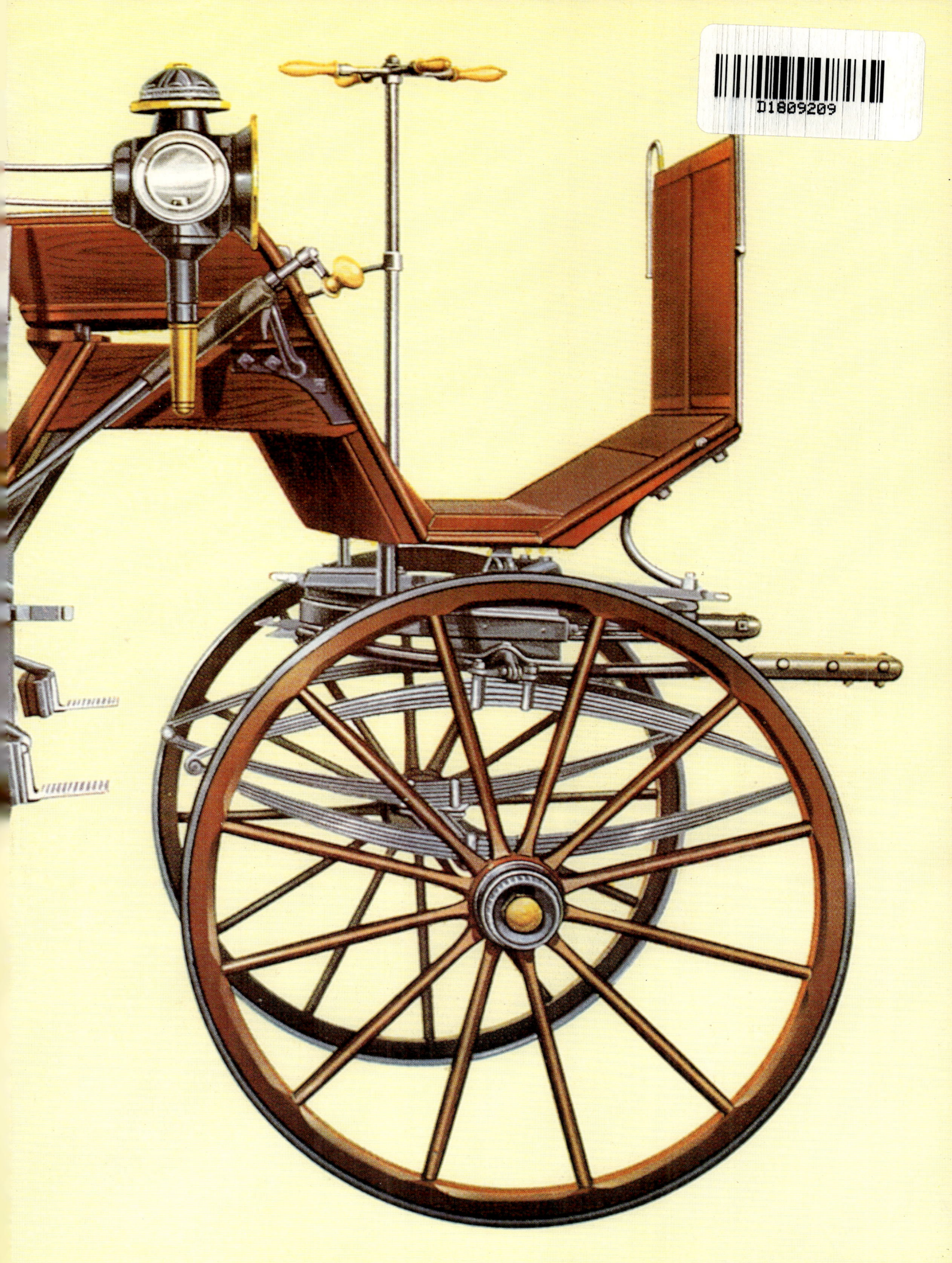

PICTURE
THE WORLD OF
CARS

PETER ROBERTS

HODDER AND STOUGHTON
LONDON SYDNEY AUCKLAND TORONTO

The publishers and author would like to express their gratitude to the following organisations and persons for their help in research and photographic documentation:

Mercedes-Benz (UK) Ltd., Daimler-Benz AG., Automobiles Citroen, Adam Opel AG., Alfa Romeo SpA., Automobiles Peugeot SA., Mr Cecil Bendall, Mr Michael Worthington-Williams, Sotheby's of London, Chrysler Corporation USA., Fiat Motor Co., Mrs Sheila Knapman and Ford GB., Ford Motor Co of Dearborn, Lips Autodron, Holland, Musée de l'Automobile Française, Porsche Cars GB., Régie Nationale des Usine Renault, Rolls-Royce Motors Ltd., Vauxhall Motors Ltd., Mr Neill Bruce, Mr Nicky Wright, Michelin Tyre Plc., Dunlop Ltd., Mr W Carter, Mr Johnny Thomas of Nantgaredig, General Motors Corporation, Bethnal Green Museum of Childhood (V & A), Volkswagenwerke AG., VAG (UK) Ltd., Lotus Group.

British Library Cataloguing in Publication Data

Roberts, Peter, 19
    Picture the world of cars.
    I. Automobiles—History—Pictorial works—
    Juvenile literature
    I. Title
    629.2'222'09   TL147
    ISBN 0-340 32747-2

Copyright © 1983 by Peter Roberts
Photographs: Peter Roberts Collection

Designed by TL Creative Services
Colour origination by Planway, London.

First published 1983

Published by Hodder and Stoughton Children's Books, a division of Hodder and Stoughton Ltd, Mill Road, Dunton Green, Sevenoaks, Kent TN13 2YJ.

Printed in Italy by New Interlitho, Milan.

front endpaper:
The first Daimler, 1886

title page:
Mercury Montego GT from USA

this page:
Lotus Esprit, 1982

back endpaper:
Rolls Royce S Spirit

CONTENTS

INTRODUCTION

The modern car was invented in Germany, first flourished in France, was further developed in America, and brought to near perfection in Britain. However, to France goes the credit for the first powered road vehicle, when Nicholas Cugnot showed his *fardier* to an astonished public. Built to the orders of Napoleon's military authorities in 1770, Cugnot's steam-driven gun-towing cart lumbered down the Paris roads just thirty-one years ahead of the next road vehicle to be made, Englishman Trevithick's steam carriage.

To France and Cugnot also goes the dubious accolade of the first road accident. He crashed his top-heavy vehicle into a garden wall!

Steam carriages made in England were the first practical self-propelled vehicles. By the 1830s they were providing a regular service on quite long journeys, as well as local routes near large cities. However, in Britain horse-drawn vehicles and railways were given legal preference, and steam road coaches quietly disappeared.

It was not until the 1880s that self-propelled road transport appeared again: much smaller vehicles and, this time, fuelled by petrol. The birthplace of the first practical cars, made by two dedicated engineers — almost at the same time and without knowing of each other's work — was Germany. Karl Benz had his workshop in Mannheim; and in Cannstatt, not far away, Gottlieb Daimler made his first vehicle.

Motor manufacturing, after a hesitant start, moved forward in giant strides. Automotive technology advanced faster than any other industry during those exciting years of the late nineteenth and early twentieth centuries, until it was outpaced a little later by the aircraft industry, whose rapid growth was forced by war.

The motor-car of today is a highly sophisticated machine, just on the threshold of harnessing the latest advances in electronics. Tomorrow's automobile, undoubtedly with new and more convenient fuels, with new systems of control and new margins of safety, will offer many new challenges, present many new problems — some are already appearing around the corner...

Opposite: Morris Oxford, 1913. This is the car with which young Bill Morris established his company. He opened for business with this model in 1913, and had sold over 1000 by the end of 1914.

André Citroën's attempt at satisfying the new market of the early 1920s, the Citroen 5CV of 1922.

MOTORING FOR THE BRAVE

German engineering partners Esslinger and Rose were worried. Their new colleague, Karl Benz, a brilliant thirty-nine-year-old designer from Karlsruhe, had been producing stationary engines for use in factories, and now he was beginning to talk wildly about making a motor vehicle — one that was pulled along the road by its own machinery!

'Nonsense, we can't waste our money on such a folly. You'll never make a vehicle work without a horse between the shafts!' said Esslinger at a company meeting in 1884.

But Karl Benz was not daunted. He had a vision of what he thought was to be the future form of road transport, and nothing was going to prevent him building the first practical horseless carriage. He persuaded a Mannheim businessman to lend him some money, and set himself up in a tiny back-street workshop, helped by his wife Bertha and his two small sons, Eugen and Richard.

Karl Benz worked long hours at his new vehicle. First he improved his own four-stroke engine, which itself was a development of his earlier two-stroke unit. Then he built around it a vehicle that was completely different from anything ever seen before. It had three bicycle-spoked wheels, and cycle-type steel tubing formed the framework. The tiny engine was at the back, and had to be started by pulling a flywheel, rather like an old-fashioned motor mower.

A local Mannheim newspaper reporter said of one of the Benz car's first public tests in 1886: 'Seldom, if ever, have passers-by in the streets of our city seen a more startling sight than on Saturday afternoon, when a one-horse chaise came…at a good clip without any horse or shafts, a man sitting under the surrey top, riding on three wheels…on his way to the centre of town. Everyone who saw him seemed

Gottlieb Daimler patented his gasoline engine in 1885 and built the first practical four-wheeled horseless carriage later that year. Its engine was a tiny 1.1 water-cooled horsepower unit.

Karl Benz, working at Mannheim in Germany, built his first motored vehicle at almost the same time as Daimler was constructing his, not far away in Cannstatt. This is the Benz Velo, an improved version of his first car.

A pioneer Panhard & Levassor, made in France in 1895, just four years after the company built France's first automobile.

Several of the first American cars looked very like a Benz Velo, as does this Whitney of 1896. But this light car is powered by a steam-driven engine, then a healthy rival to the internal-combustion motor.

The first Cadillac, made in 1903 at Detroit. A single-cylinder machine, simple and crude, the Model A was the forerunner of the highest quality line of cars produced in America.

unable to grasp what they had before their eyes and the astonishment was general and widespread.'

But general interest was slight. And, too, the police disapproved of such a fearsome vehicle on the horse-packed roads of the day. As the speed limit was fixed at four miles an hour, what good was a vehicle that could do a breathtaking 10 mph?

Karl Benz, as wily as he was inventive, invited the Minister of the Interior of Baden for a test ride. He had previously had a quiet word with the local milkman, who used a small horse-drawn cart for his daily round. When the little open three-wheeler car was chugging along at its maximum permitted speed, the milkman's horse trotted past and the milkman jeered good-naturedly from his float at the crawling motor vehicle. Then he did it again. At the third encounter with the milkman, the Minister told Benz to get a move on.

'But the regulations, Herr Minister?'

'Hang the regulations!' cried the Minister — and the speed limit in the Grand Duchy of Baden was thereupon raised.

First long-distance drive

One Sunday morning in 1888, Eugen Benz suggested to his mother that, as father was away at an exhibition, they take the now-improved three-wheeler to Pforzheim, a town about seventy miles south of Mannheim, where her family lived. So Frau Bertha Benz and her two sons set off on the world's first long-distance car journey.

Eugen took the tiller and Richard sat in the 'emergency seat', ready to jump out to fetch water or to help push the car up gradients. Petrol was purchased from an apothecary (chemist) on the route, and at the village of Bauschlott a cobbler fashioned a new leather pad for their brakes. But when they stopped at lunchtime, a frightened innkeeper refused to serve them a meal.

Minor repairs were successfully made by the two boys several times, and at dusk they arrived at the Post-Hotel at Pforzheim, too tired to go calling on their relatives that evening. A crowd soon gathered outside the hotel, full of awe and admiration for the crew of this strange vehicle…

Karl Benz was by now selling his cars to the public. He had first designed the Viktoria, his first four-wheeled car; and then on 1st April 1894 he exhibited his new Velo, a scaled-down Viktoria of simpler design, to be made in large numbers. The Benz Velo, made for customers who needed a cheaper vehicle than the Viktoria, soon became the most popular car of its time, and Benz the most successful car maker of his day.

The Cannstatt challenge

Meanwhile, down the road at Cannstatt, some sixty miles away from the Benz factory, lived and worked another German motor engineering pioneer, Gottlieb Daimler. He was also developing his first motor vehicle in his small workshop at exactly the same time as Benz, although neither knew the other was engaged on a similar project!

Daimler had installed his first half-horsepower engine in a sort of skeletal motor-cycle and tried it out privately in the yard of his works, with encouraging success. His aim, although similar to that of Benz, was to make engines that could power a variety of vehicles, on land or water, or even

Frenchman Armand Peugeot, son of a family of ironmongers and cycle-makers, made his first gasoline automobile in 1891, using a Daimler engine made by Panhard & Levassor of Paris. This is a 1902 Peugeot, still in fine condition, on a London-to-Brighton Commemoration Run.

This must have been a common scene in early motoring days!

Another American car that has stood that test of time, the Oldsmobile. This is Ransom Olds' 'Merry Oldsmobile', the 1901 Curved Dash machine. The little high-wheeled motorised buggy was the first-ever car to be made by a form of mass-production.

in the air. He immediately tried to modify his 1885 'single track' vehicle for use as a motor sled, with less success. He decided to try again, this time with four wheels on the ground.

Daimler ordered a light coach from a Stuttgart company, telling them — and all his friends — that he wanted its delivery kept secret as it was to be a surprise for his wife's birthday. The coach was duly despatched to Daimler's works, an engine was fitted, and the vehicle trundled out into the works yard for testing.

Soon after that, helped by his seventeen-year-old son Paul, and his brilliant assistant Willi Maybach, Daimler built a two-cylinder motor, much more powerful and reliable than the original. Then they built a motor-powered rail vehicle; a mobile saw; a fire engine; a street car; a dozen marine motors; and an engine for an early airship.

The airship, built in 1888 by a Leipzig bookseller, was in fact a dirigible balloon, but when Daimler's 2 hp unit was used to drive its horizontal and vertical propellers, it magically became a vehicle that could be driven in whatever direction its pilot wished to go, rather than depending entirely on the whims of the breeze. This crude airship flew four kilometres on its maiden voyage. Daimler had achieved his second objective — using his engine for travel through the air....

By 1889 Daimler had designed his famous Steelwheeler — an open two-seater car which broke away completely

Early automotive humour, French style. Barred routes made no difference to the Barré car, it seemed. G. Barré, of Niort in France, made modestly-priced cars from 1900 to 1930.

from horse-and-carriage form. He took it to the Paris Exposition. He illuminated his stand with electric lights driven by one of the engines, and there the high spoke-wheeled car caught the eye of a woman who was to become the keystone of the French motor industry.

The car comes to France

Madame Sarazin's husband had died two years earlier, and her present escort was engineer Émile Levassor of Panhard and Levassor, a machinery firm near Paris. Before his death Monsieur Sarazin had made an agreement with Daimler to build and sell his engines under licence in France. Sarazin had commissioned Levassor to produce several experimental units for testing before he died. Now, the Paris world fair brought Daimler, Levassor and the widow Sarazin together.

The lady had earlier persuaded the German motor maker to honour his agreement with her late husband, and now with the skilled engineer Levassor at her side, the time was right to offer a motor vehicle to the French nation. Levassor married Mme Sarazin in 1890, and the firm of Panhard & Levassor made its first motor-car for the country that was soon to become the leading motoring nation of the world.

The first P & L was a mid-engined buggy with seats for four, two of which were right on top of the hot, smoky engine. Levassor soon changed the layout, putting the engine in the front, and then the clutch, followed by an open-to-the-weather gearbox, and final-drive to the road wheels. He unconsciously decided the 'drive-layout' of the standard motor-car for the next half-a-dozen decades — until modern times in fact, for it is only recently that popular use of front-wheel-drive (instead of rear drive) has modified the pattern of the everyday car. Thus France took the lead in the automobile world, and Germany dropped back to second place in the race to establish the infant motor industry.

If 'motoring' Germany was falling behind France, Britain was still solidly in the horse age, with half-a-dozen regulations that put using a motor-car on public roads right on the sharp edge of the law. The maximum speed through towns was 2 mph, and in the country just 4 mph. In addition motor vehicles required 'three persons in attendance' whilst the fearsome machine was in motion… Britain, therefore, could only boast perhaps half-a-dozen horseless carriages throughout the land, in the early 1890s.

English law was not to be hurried, and it wasn't until 1896 that motors were allowed to travel at speeds of up to 12 mph. And this was when on the Continent speeds of up to 80 mph were reached during competitions on the open

15

road! It took a small but powerful coterie of rich sportsmen, and the heir to the throne — the Prince of Wales himself — to persuade society to accept the new motoring. The delay meant that Britain joined the motor-making business some ten years behind the rest of Europe.

Enter the USA

The United States of America was even farther behind the leaders than Britain, but was about to move into motoring with explosive energy.

There had been a few early experimental motor road vehicles in the United States, most of them steam-driven or electrical buggies, but it was 1893 before the USA's sixty-three million people began to realise that they need not depend entirely for transportation on the twenty million horses then in use. When American piano manufacturer William Steinway and Gottlieb Daimler contracted to sell the latter's engines, Americans began to hear about the Steel-wheeler and its amazing ability to carry passengers without a horse. Then at the World Exhibition in Chicago, the first Daimler cars were shown.

Benz had also been demonstrating his car in the USA and had captured a lot of publicity. In fact, it was a Benz-based vehicle that is considered to be America's first successful home-produced automobile, made by the brothers Duryea of Springfield, Massachusetts, in 1893.

News of the first 'motor contest' from Paris to Rouen in 1894 fired the imagination of the editor of the Chicago *Times Herald*, and he decided to mount a motor race, the

Tricars were popular in Britain in the early days of motoring. This is a 1904 Rexette, a three-wheeler with the passenger seat 'nearest the accident', and most of its 5 hp engine under the driver's seat. Made in Birmingham.

De Dion Bouton, another early French marque. Count de Dion teamed up with boiler-maker Georges Bouton to make steam cars and tricycles in 1883, moving over to petrol vehicles ten years later. This is a 1904 wagonnette.

The proud owner of a 1905 Ford C Model is about to take a morning spin in his fringed Surrey. The engine was still under-floor at this time and the car has a dummy bonnet (hood).

This Renault limousine, already distinguishable by its coal-scuttle front, was just the vehicle for Madame's morning ride around the Bois de Boulogne. Protected by the glassed-in cab, modelled on a railway carriage, and drawn by the 20.30 hp motor, this was the elegant way to travel in 1906.

first such contest in the USA, 'to encourage the improvement of the horseless carriage'. The brave new world of America soon caught on to the new mobility. Highwheeled horse-buggies had been the main form of transport up to the turn of the century, but now doctors and drummers (travelling salesmen), the most mobile men in society, began to buy the first spidery buggy-like automobiles.

Backyard mechanics spent long hours in the woodshed, hammering out America's first cars. Their cars, though, were rather like ships in a desert, for the great continent of North America was almost without roads! Most paved or metalled roads dwindled to cart-tracks just outside town. So while Britain had its anti-motoring laws, the United States had its own handicaps of deep dusty ruts, or winter mud up to the axles. Cars similar to the well-tried American buggies were needed — high off the ground, light but strong. Those characteristics were the basis of the early American car: cars that could take a battering from the roads and tracks and still manage to survive in working order.

Farmer's boy Ford

Farmer's boy Henry Ford built a little two-cylinder engine made from gas-piping and bicycle parts, and put it in a box-like car. And it ran — after Ford had axed down the woodshed doorpost to get it out on the road! After a couple of false starts in business Ford finally formed his motor empire, the Ford Motor Company, in 1903 — although the official advice to motorists of the day read: 'If a horse is unwilling to pass an automobile, the driver should take it apart and quickly conceal the parts in the bushes'!

Other automobile companies were formed daily. Ransom Olds had been making cars since 1896 at Lansing, Michigan, when a factory fire destroyed all but one prototype model, the Curved Dash Oldsmobile, which was intended to be part of a range of vehicles. The 'Merry Olds', as the Curved Dash was often called, was a simple affair with two underfloor cylinders, slow-revving at 'one chug per telegraph pole'. By 1902 the Curved Dash, the factory's single remaining product, was selling like hot cakes. This little pram-like car was tough enough to be driven safely by the simplest cowhand. It became the first car in the United States to be mass-produced, pre-dating the Ford system by several years.

Detroit was the melting pot for many other great companies during this founding period of the American automobile industry. Henry Leland, gunmaker and perfectionist, took over the first of Ford's companies (then failing badly), worked hard, talked some enthusiasm into it, and renamed it Cadillac.

Back in Europe those first exciting years of the twentieth century showed that a new era was indeed in the making. In France Louis Renault, young, dour, and as brilliant a businessman as he was mechanic, had drilled and hammered away in his own backyard (annoying the neighbours in the quiet Paris suburb of Billancourt) to great effect. His first little car, a light four-wheeler based on the earlier De Dion tricycle, attracted a dozen orders on that first momentous Christmas Eve in 1898 when he showed it to his friends. A few short years later Louis and his brothers had become Europe's leading popular car maker. France was by this time the world's largest producer, making more than 30,000 motor vehicles in 1903.

The German milestone

In Germany both Benz and Daimler had flourished. Opel, too, were rapidly gaining stature. A company that had previously made sewing machines and bicycles, it was now in the automobile field, making its own complete car by 1902 at Russelsheim near Frankfurt.

An event that occurred at Nice in the south of France one March day in 1901 changed the face of the motoring world. This was the appearance of a new Daimler, called Mercedes, after the young daughter of Daimler's French representative. When the first Mercedes showed its paces it astonished the knowledgeable crowds gathered for the sporting week at Nice. Long, low, fast, silent — it also shocked every other motor manufacturer to the core. Overnight their latest models became old-fashioned. Suspension, gears, brakes, cooling, engine function — all were so vastly improved that the new Mercedes suddenly became the most wanted car in the world...

A German miracle. The Mercedes, first seen at Nice in the spring of 1901, was one of the major milestones in motoring history. Its advanced technology rendered every other car of the day obsolete.

England, too, was making motor-cars for Edwardian society.
This Wolseley-Siddeley of 1906 was equally luxurious inside its
richly upholstered cab; but, as usual, the paid driver was given
very little weather protection.

Michelin were pioneers, with
Dunlop, of pneumatic tyres.

MICHELIN-GLEITSCHUTZ
MIT GEPANZERTER DOPPELSOHLE

DEUTSCHE MICHELIN - PNEUMATIK
AKTIENGESELLSCHAFT
FRANKFURT A·M·

TIN LIZZIE TO SIERRA

Most people would agree that Henry Ford became the most important man in the American automotive industry. His dependable and cheap transport started with the Model T Ford in 1908. Although the story of the American Ford — and later Ford cars made in other countries — had its successes and its setbacks, there was nothing to beat the Model T for sheer value for money at the time of its launch, and for several years afterwards, particularly as the price was lowered several times.

1 October 1908 was the day the world first saw the squared-up open car. 'Homely as a burro and useful as a pair of shoes,' said the press. With its light, strong frame of vanadium steel; its 20 hp engine; a gear-change system that even the simplest mid-western farmer could operate; its high 26 cm road clearance (it needed it on American tracks) — the Ford T would do a rattling 45 mph. The 'Tin Lizzie', as the Model T was called, was used for every imaginable mechanical purpose. With attachments it could milk cows, saw wood, uproot trees. It soon became so popular that after a few months' production, Ford sent a panic telegram to all his dealers 'Do not send any more orders until advised by this office.' He just couldn't cope with the rush!

Henry Ford bought rubber plantations, mines and railways to enable him to continue to supply his popular car. He had one aim: to provide the ordinary man with transport of his own. He even refused to become a candidate for the presidency of the United States in 1923, so dedicated was he to his work.

And in many ways that has been the continuing story of the Ford 'empire', which has now spread to the ends of the earth.

The Model A succeeded the T in 1928. Britain saw the little Type Y in 1933 — the £100 Ford — and the V8 Pilot in 1948. The US factories turned out model after model, including the sportive Thunderbird and the Falcon. A co-operative effort by Britain and America brought the Ford GT 40 to the race circuits, with wins at Le Mans in the 1960s. The UK has had Anglias, Prefects, the enormously popular Cortinas and Capris, and now Escorts, Fiestas and the Sierra.

Ford launched his legendary Model T in 1908, and manufactured it for some eighteen years. Over 15 million examples were rolled off the assembly lines, supplying much of the world with its first mechanical transportation. This is a 1914 Model T Ford.

This British advertisement of 1917 explains the joys of Ford ownership to the country-dweller!

A Ford model with Lincoln connections, the Mercury was designed to rival the Oldsmobile and Buick. This 1972 GT Montego Coupé was very similar to a scaled-down Lincoln Continental, and had a choice of engines of up to 7 litres.

Model T, about 1924, with a lively party of French holidaymakers about to exhibit their car in a Concours d'Elégance, a competition for the best-kept car.

The '£100 Ford'. On sale in Britain by 1933, this little 8 hp Ford Type Y helped first-time buyers to enter the world of motoring.

The Ford Fiesta, small car of the late seventies. The British company threw out all their old designs when they made this model, with its front-wheel drive and high-compression transverse engine.

Launched in 1962, the Ford Cortina set the pattern for a whole range of inexpensive family cars for the following 20 years. This is the Mark I model.

Latest in the long Ford line is the Sierra. Wind-tunnel testing has given the car a look of the 1990s, and its balanced layout gives the car a safe performance under all conditions.

CARRIAGES FOR GENTLEMEN

Burners and pressure gauges abound on the dashboard of this Stanley Steamer built by the Stanley Brothers (who once ran a photographic factory) from Newton, Massachusetts, USA. The boiler of this model had a working pressure of twenty-seven times normal atmosphere. Small wonder that some passsengers were eager for their journey to be over . . .

Around 1905 hundreds of small motor companies began to spring up. The world had by then heard of the motor-car. Most people had actually seen several, and the fear of the 'nasty explosion machines' had begun to recede as more appeared puttering along the dusty highways of Europe and America.

New firms, some that made only a couple of dozen vehicles a year, offered electric cars, steamers, water-cooled combustion engines and air-cooled units, including some that were air-cooled for winter use and could be switched over to water-cooling in the summer. Some advertisements claimed that their products could 'make thirty miles an hour' (optimistic this, for many); some assured the public that their cars ran noiselessly. Electric car makers made much of their ease of starting—'even ladies can do it'; and steam companies emphasised the silence and safety of their vehicles.

Motorists in those early days had to be more than mere drivers, for the bits and pieces that fell off, fractured, bent, burst or just plain wore out, were legion. Tyres were frail, and on the rutted and flinty roads of the day they were not expected to last more than a couple of thousand miles, and were certainly not expected to survive more than a morning's spin without a puncture.

Dust was a real problem. The roads of Europe and other continents were designed for leisurely horse transport, too slow in their progress to raise much dust. But the vacuum-cleaner effect of a swiftly passing motor vehicle threw vast columns of choking dust into the clean air of the countryside, and into the atmosphere of residential areas, turning the washday whites to grey!

Advice to early motorists

Much advice on how to drive a motor-car was given in magazines and newspapers. One London journal said: 'Always keep to your right side, for in all probability you will find some other vehicle coming towards you from the opposite direction!' The fact that in Britain 'right' is left, must have considerably confused some learner drivers!

Another piece of wise advice read: 'However fond you are of the lady, disaster will result if you endeavour to steer with one hand and embrace her with the other.'

There were, of course, some drivers who caused more trouble than others. Dust-raising drivers were one thing, more the fault of the roads than the motorist, but horse-scaring scorchers and chicken-killing cads were another—as were those maniacs whose speed sometimes exceeded 20 mph, the limit for many countries during the first decade of the twentieth century. Dozens of 'furious driving' cases were brought before the courts by the police, and many were fined £2 for speeding at 30 mph. Another popular way of adding to the court's revenue was a five-shilling (25p) fine for blown-out carbide lamps.

Cars were rapidly becoming more familiar. By 1905 in England there were about 5000 people to every car. This meant that if you lived in London you would be quite accustomed to seeing motor-cars, taxis and lorries chugging around Hyde Park Corner, but if you lived in Dover or Hull you might not have seen any.

In the USA there were just 8000 automobile registrations in 1900, but by 1905 there had been a great surge of 'automobilism' and 77,000 new cars were on the road. In Germany and France, too, the auto was beginning to take its place as a useful tool of society. In France Panhard was perhaps the leading make, with Mors and Peugeot close behind. De Dion Bouton and Renault were making vehicles for everyday use—from taxis and tricars (threewheelers) to road sprinklers and delivery vans. The luxury market was headed by the Delauney-Belleville, by 1908 a smooth-running 6-cylinder model.

The 'Best Car in the World'

About this time the French Panhard was also being sold in England by a young man of good family, the Hon Charles Rolls. Charles had been a rebel since before he went to school. He was a science buff and a motoring enthusiast. His London showrooms were attracting customers, but he wanted to be able to sell a British machine that was better than the French cars he was forced to offer. Sadly he concluded there were none.

But the Hon Charles was wrong. Henry Royce, a cranemaker in Manchester, had bought a French Decauville, sniffed at its poor engineering and finish, taken it to pieces, and put it back together, adding a number of his own ideas. The new car was ready on 1 April

A British Daimler 'Detachable' of 1905. The roof and upper sides of this car could be winched off (and hung from the garage roof) transforming the vehicle into an open tourer.

One of Opel's successful early models, the Doppel Phaeton of 1909, with all the style of an Edwardian carriage waiting for its mistress. This one was a four-seater, four-cylinder tourer that could reach a speed of 60 kilometres an hour.

1904, and Royce took it out for a trial run.

When he invited some newspapermen for a ride, their language was lyrical. 'When the engine is running,' said *The Times* joyfully, 'one can neither hear nor feel it, and pedestrians never seem to hear the car's approach.' Compared with the Royce, with its quiet tickover, its smooth springing, 'all others sound like an avalanche of tea-trays' reported the newspaper.

Royce had started his working life as a local farmer's scarecrow, rising to the job of newspaperboy. He had led a hard life, underfed, under-privileged, only irregularly attending school. But his opportunity came when, at 14, he became a railway engineering apprentice, later moving to an electric light company. These two working experiences, and his own burning desire to make a first-class job of anything he encountered, led him to the ownership of an established business by the time he was forty.

The following year Rolls and Royce joined forces. By the opening of the 1906 Motor Show a Rolls-Royce 40/50, later to be called the Silver Ghost, was ready to be launched. The car was made until 1925, and during its lifetime was bought by kings, princes and presidents the world over, truly earning the title of 'Best Car in the World'.

The car changes shape

The appearance of the car was now changing rapidly. Although the layout, with some exceptions, had become similar to that of today's automobiles, the super-structure—the body-shape—was just beginning to develop along more functional lines. Speeds had increased, so cars now needed windscreens. The tonneau, with a rear door that deposited passengers into the muddy road, was replaced by the side entrance which faced the pavement. This was made easier by the fact that chassis were getting longer and suspensions lower. Six-cylinder engines, now popular in up-market models, helped bring about this change too, as the engines needed a longer front-end to accommodate them. Running boards, sidescreens, doors and—by 1910—scuttles or cowls that moulded the rear of the bonnet into the design of the body and covered the exposed dashboard, were also introduced. A few years later the first 'torpedoes' made their debut. They were open touring-type cars with a straight line from the front of the bonnet to the rear of the car. These paved the way for the clean-lined open tourers and sports-tourers of the 1920s. Mudguards, too, changed shape from great plough-like blades to more wheel-hugging contours. Some were even made as part of the body-panel moulding, anticipating the designs of up to thirty years later.

Another advance in those tranquil Edwardian days was the detachable wheel rim. What a relief to the puncture-prone motorist! Now he could just jack the car up and fix on a spare rim and tyre, using eight bolts to secure it to the wheel. Early motorists had been forced to remove old tyres with crude, spoon-like tools, usually tearing their finger-nails and severely pinching their hands in the process. Now this new detachable rim greatly eased the hardship of motoring. Another innovation—a modest electrical gadget for starting the engine—appeared on the Cadillac, and was destined to change the entire face of motoring. The self-starter appeared in 1912. Before that motorists had to go

From the sunny side of the Alps, a 1909 Fiat. This large Italian family-type tourer had a four-cylinder motor and could lope along at a respectable speed. It still does, having covered many thousands of miles in recent years.

A glimpse of the Rolls-Royce Silver Ghost 40/50 hp, first seen clad in its shining aluminium bodywork at the London Motor Show in 1906.

The English company of Alldays & Onions built this sturdy Edwardian long-legged tourer known for its reliability — but not for its efficient weather protection!

The young man's dream of open-air motoring, 1910. This Renault sported a two-cylinder motor under its coal-scuttle bonnet.

Town Carriage, 1910. This Austin 'city car' had a central steering wheel for (so it was thought) better driver vision on both sides of the car in town traffic of Edwardian days.

through the wrist-twisting performance of swinging the starting handle to fire an often reluctant, and always heavy, engine. Heaving over the handle of a little one-cylinder De Dion Bouton may not have caused any slipped discs, but try turning over the six bucket-sized cylinders of a 70 hp Delaunay-Belleville at your peril!

Ladies in gear!

The electric self-starter was a boon to all. It was developed from the mechanism of a cash-register, in which the battery gives one big slam of current to open the drawer. The self-starter also introduced a whole new section of society to motoring—women. Once lady drivers could cope with cold-starting by merely pressing a little button, they began to take car driving seriously.

Soon the ladies started to change their style of dress. Swirling skirts and ribbons a-flying in the breeze got in the way of the gear levers and pedals. When our great-grandmothers began to wear their skirts shorter (they had been worn to ground level for hundreds of years), ladies began to drive out alone—an unheard-of thing until the end of the Edwardian era.

Advice to this brave band was legion. Other female pioneers would suggest in ladies' magazines that: 'If you are to drive alone on the highways...it is advisable to carry a small revolver. I have an automatic colt and find it easy to handle as there is practically no recoil... A mask for the upper part of the face and the eyes if you wish to keep your skin protected from the stinging grit that you will surely encounter.' Then for those who had rings on their fingers...'One should remove one's rings, especially if they are set with precious stones, before taking the wheel. Most roads will cause such a vibration about the hands that the stones will rattle loose and be lost.' Pistols—and masks—these were the popular female accessories: pistols for bodily protection and masks for facial protection against the hostile elements.

The Morris Oxford was one of the first genuine British light cars. Its modest price and sturdy build helped to attract young buyers away from the gimcrack cyclecar offering of the day.

One of the last single-cylinder De Dion Boutons, this 1911 two-seater 8 hp had a fold-down 'dickey seat' at the rear with room for two passengers who did not object to some draughty travel!

Beginnings of mass-production

Cars were advertised for sale in society magazines, both in new and used condition. Although 'motoring for the masses' was some years away from the early part of the twentieth century, numbers of quite modest vehicles were made and offered. In 1905 a 9 hp Vauxhall could be bought for £220; a Clyde of 12 hp for £250; a new Humber, compact and neat, for £315. In the second-hand market one could find such exciting advertisements as 'Metallurgique 12-14 hp 1909 model, racy two-seater body, scuttle dash, low hood, windscreen, Stepney wheel, complete set of lamps, excellent tyres, just overhauled, £250. Seen in London.'

One large advertisement offered, back in 1903:

Panhard Car 40 hp, (Paris-Berlin) type tonneau body, £1,100

Automotor car 10 hp, latest style tonneau body, £260

Mercedes Car 16-20 hp, 4 cylinders, 2 bodies (tonneau and limousine), £670

Orient Express 6 hp, splendid condition, solid tyres...£60

De Dion Voiturette 6 hp, hood and glass and all improvements...£100

Gladiator Racing Car 20 hp, (Paris-Vienna) 100 kilos an hour...£235

AUTOMOBILE COMPONENTS LTD, 18-24 Church Street, Islington, London.

That little list would be worth a king's ransom now, particularly the Panhard and the Gladiator, which were copies of the type used in the great races of the 'heroic' age of motoring—the 1901 Paris to Berlin race and the 1902 Paris-Vienna marathon.

By 1909 the balance of the motoring 'population' had changed surprisingly. France, for almost twenty years the

Opel Torpedo, 1912. This tidy little two-seater housed a big 2 litre engine of four cylinders. At this time Opel of Russelsheim, near Frankfurt in Germany, was enjoying great racing success, and had already made its first aero-engine.

automotive leader of the European nations, had taken second place to Britain, with almost 90,000 cars on the road to some 35,000 registered in France. And British designs were improving rapidly. Chain-drive—cumbersome, noisy and often unreliable—had almost totally given way to a shaft-drive very like that in many cars today. Engines had become much neater, with their vital oil supplies carried through drilled internal ducts rather than along a spaghetti network of fragile copper pipes draped over the outside of the engine. Motor-building was becoming a really important industry, with parts being made in large numbers, and assembly lines replacing groups of workers building a single entire vehicle.

Motor manufacturers had been given a jolt—and a lesson—when in 1908 three Cadillac cars demonstrated high quality coupled with accurate mass-production. During the American Civil War the northern states had introduced the practice of mass-producing rifle parts instead of carefully filing and fitting each part to its special mate for every separate weapon. Cadillac boss Henry Leland, whose motto was 'Craftsmanship a creed, accuracy a law', adopted this principle in his automotive work.

At England's new Brooklands racing circuit, three Model K Cadillacs were tried out at speed. Then under the watchful eye of Britain's Royal Automobile Club the three cars were taken completely apart, the pieces scrambled thoroughly, and put back together again. The test proved beyond doubt that mass-made parts could be engineered so accurately that any one part would fit any other mate. This meant that motor parts could be manufactured separately, away from the final assembly area, thus speeding up the business of making the complete car. The watchers went away, applied the system—and the world's mobility took another leap forward.

USA's 2000 manufacturers

In the United States there were, by 1912, almost 2000 different automobile makers, some of whom built one a month or one a week—or, like Ford, nearly 200,000 a year. Oldsmobile and Buick were flourishing: Buick had sold over 11,000 of its sturdy Model 10 (price new $1050 in 1910); Oldsmobile was offering its legendary Limited, a great six-cylinder touring car with huge 42 inch wheels, large enough in diameter to iron out the roughest backwoods track. Cadillac, too, and Hudson, were selling well at home and overseas, but the demand for steam cars from White and Stanley was now on the wane.

Advertisements were becoming more sophisticated. 'Have you a Clark auto-heater for your car?' queried one, while the Moline from Illinois offered its own (not very good) non-electric starter.

Stoddard Dayton's phrase 'That's the next car I buy' was designed to guide the buyer towards what the makers considered to be the perfect car. And R.E. Olds, who now made the Reo car, flatly stated that his 1912 product was the best he—or anyone else—could do: 'The car that marks my limit', boasted his ads. The air-cooled Franklin had a good selling point with its 'Nothing to freeze, nothing to boil' and 'We've done away with the plumbing!' catch phrases.

The Franklin was, in fact, a very popular make, with its no-fuss engine and the advanced suspension which gave a smooth ride. Franklin, from Syracuse, NY, made efficient

Another classic British car, the Prince Henry Vauxhall, vintage 1914. Considered one of the world's first true sports-cars, this 4 litre (the first ones were 3 litre) was the direct ancestor of the famous sporting Vauxhall 30/98.

A handsome example of a Boat-Tail Tourer from the French sporting marque of Delage. It was made in 1925, when luxury sports-cars that looked like speedboats were the fashion. Some even had small ships' ventilators to complete the illusion!

Air-cooled Opera Coupé. The Franklin from USA used a highly successful air-cooled engine for over thirty years. It was the most successful engine of its type until the Volkswagen Beetle appeared after World War II.

Still best in the world. However, this Rolls-Royce Silver Ghost of 1920, at a chassis price of £2200, was already getting a little elderly and was to be replaced by the Phantom I in 1925.

air-cooled cars until 1934, when they turned to helicopter engines—which seemed a natural development.

In Germany, Benz and Daimler were rivals for the 'carriage trade', whilst Opel were scooping up the sporting silverware, forging a reputation through motor sport successes. Opel built their first aircraft in 1911, spurred on by the German government, and had started making military trucks a year earlier.

The cycle-car

This was the period of the so-called 'new motoring', particularly in France. Motor manufacturers, and others, saw a new market in the young enthusiasts who could never afford a real full-size car but were longing to have something—anything—with an engine and (unlike a motorcycle) a couple of seats. The cycle-car was invented. Cycle-cars of lightweight design usually meant crudity of construction—and crudity of handling. In Europe hundreds of spindly, light car confections appeared, with wheels and engines where one would least expect them and makeshift mechanics of wire-and-bobbin. These ran on the same fine straight roads of the Continent as the majestic carriages such as Belgium's Metallurgique, Italy's Isotta-Fraschini, and France's regal Delaunay-Belleville. In Britain light Humberettes and Waverleys vied with great Daimlers (British-made version, and by appointment to the Royal Family).

The man in the street did not yet expect to have a genuine car in his garage, and for a while he was satisfied with a humble Bedelia, GN, Morgan or a Wall Tricar. Indeed, as a motoring journalist of the day said 'The cycle-car fever grew, between 1910 and 1912, into a cycle-car disease.' But it all vanished in the smoke of a war that changed the face of motoring and society...

WORKING WHEELS

For ploughed fields, mountain tracks or battlefields, there is nothing like a four-wheel drive vehicle. Every road wheel is powered by the engine, and every deep-treaded tyre works to keep the vehicle moving, no matter how tough the terrain. Perhaps that is why the four-wheel drive vehicle was first used seriously for wartime work.

Just after World War I the American army decided that a small go-anywhere vehicle was needed to replace the horse. It had to be light so that it could be manhandled. It had to have a low profile for work in the front line. It had to have strong towing power to haul weapons and equipment into battle. The Jeep fulfilled these needs.

Whilst the Jeep was not the first true cross-country vehicle (Citroën had made several for safari work twenty years earlier), this military dodge-about was the first to be made in large numbers for use as a general workhorse. Made by Ford and Willys of America, Jeeps (from the initials GP—General Purpose) had a magnificent Second World War record as fast, front-line transportation; as ambulances; as 'liberty wagons'; even as railcars, using flanged wheels and run on local railways.

Today Jeeps and other similar rough-ride vehicles are used for less warlike jobs. The British Land Rover has had huge success, particularly in newly-developed countries where roads are poor, and on ranches and farms. The later Range Rover four-wheel-drive vehicle is used for police work; for rescue operations and other jobs in rough terrain where ordinary cars cannot travel; and a thousand other daily tasks.

No desert or jungle safari is complete without a Range Rover. When it was first seen in 1970 buyers queued for the privilege of buying one. This is a special version with six wheels for even greater traction.

Working wheels in Italy's Alpine region. This four-wheel-drive Fiat seems to have had no bother in getting up to mountain goat altitude.

Today four-wheel-drive vehicles are popular for on-the-road journeys as well as for rough terrain. Many motor makers who had previously produced conventional cars are now in the cross-country field, and these rugged vehicles are now seen parked outside town houses. This is a Rancho, from Matra of France.

Still with something of the Jeep look, the Dihatsu Fourtrack from Japan is often seen in holiday regions, hired out to visitors who wish to be mobile on their vacation. It has four-wheel drive and either a petrol or diesel engine.

First of the line, go-anywhere Jeep, in wartime dress — right down to the roll of barbed wire on the front end.

Jeep Cherokee. By the 1970s the spartan war-proved vehicle had been developed to this luxury level. This 2-ton six-seater has a 4288 cc motor and is powerful enough to see off most of today's sports-cars.

THE GREAT RACE

The long straight road south from Poitiers to Angoulême passes through a little town called Ruffec. There, in France's Charente region, where vines and vegetables swathe the countryside, the busy autoroute to the south of France now bypasses the town. But one night, long ago, Ruffec was on the route of an historic journey. The first-ever motor race took place over a two-day period from Paris to Bordeaux in 1895, an event that created a new sport . . .

The time is 3.30 am on Thursday, 12 June 1895. The long straight main street is empty. Emile Levassor, whom we have already met, is driving his own car. He set off from Paris just after midday and has been travelling non-stop. Here at Ruffec, some 400 kms on, he has arranged to change places with a No 2 driver, who will take the Panhard-Levassor two-seater on to Bordeaux, turn round, and drive back to Ruffec. Levassor, duly rested, will then take over and conduct the car to Paris.

However, the tireless and single-minded Levassor has travelled so fast, and is so far ahead of schedule, that his relief driver is still in bed! Levassor decides to continue at the wheel, and drives on through the small hours, his candle-lamps flickering in the darkness as he rumbles and rattles over the dusty road to the coast.

He reaches Bordeaux at 10.30 next morning, drinks a glass of champagne, and ten minutes later is on his way back to Paris. Passing Ruffec again, he sees that this time his relief *pilote* is ready and eager to take over the wheel. But Emile, who has now been on the road for some thirty hours, waves him away. He is not going to risk losing the enormous lead he has built up over the other competitors.

Levassor arrived in Paris 48 hours and 48 minutes after he started: an average speed of about 15 mph over the 732-mile route — not quite as fast as a relay of cyclists could cover the distance. But in those far-off days the car was a strange new invention. It had never been used in a speed

PARIS-VIENNE 1902

FARMAN sur PANHARD

The greatest of the early 'pioneer' races was the Paris-Vienna marathon of 1902. Marcel Renault won this event in his small car, against the finest (and largest) competition cars the world could produce.

This Daimler, made in Cannstatt, Germany, in 1899 was the forerunner of the first Mercedes, which startled the sporting world in 1901 by its advanced performance.

competition, and no man had ever driven a vehicle for such a length of time. No engine had been put to this test before...

The Paris-Bordeaux event was a truly amazing feat for Levassor and his car. The odd fact is that he was disqualified after winning the race — for having only two seats in the car instead of four. But history, as you may have guessed, took little notice of that, and Levassor's success has been proudly recorded in the annals of motoring.

Motor sport soon became popular in Europe and the USA. By 1895 the USA had mounted its first race, in the Chicago area, a puffing and slithering contest of about 55 miles through November snows and ice.

Serious racing started in the USA with the first of the Vanderbilt Cup series in 1904: races which must have had something of the atmosphere of the Monaco Grand Prix. Certainly the Vanderbilt Cup, held in and out of the residential districts of Long Island, soon became the social event of the year, with parties of onlookers picnicking by the roadside.

The capital-to-capital races

Meanwhile in Europe racing between the capital cities of various countries became a great attraction. The long haul from Paris to Vienna in 1902 proved to be the most dramatic event of the time.

This was a race in true heroic style. Long, even by today's standards, the 1050-mile route started at Champigny Hill outside Paris and went through France to Belfort near the Swiss frontier. From Belfort, through Switzerland to Bregenz, race competitors had to hold their positions, as the Swiss government did not permit racing.

The last great race before the first world war was the French Grand Prix of 1914. This is the 4.5 litre car in which German driver Christian Lautenschalger won the event using team tactics for the first time.

The international sporting world of 1910, as seen by a Bosch poster.

De Dietrich, 1905. This historic French two-seater racing car of the 'heroic' days of speed contests is still in working order. During the last war it was cut in half and hidden from the invading German army. The joins can still be seen. Engine, 5.4 litres; four cylinders; water-cooled. Top speed today, over 55 mph.

Crossing the Austrian border the race was on again, next stop Salzburg. From there, along a relatively fast road to the dazzling city of Vienna, the competitors were to make a final dash.

A huge crowd of 50,000 watched 117 cars leave the starting-line. First the heavyweights departed in a cloud of dust — the 70 hp Panhards, the massive Mors, the Mercedes cars — followed by the smaller, slower vehicles — the Renaults, Decauvilles, and so on, right down to a Laurin-Klement motored bicycle.

The stories of this race are legion. It is said that the British driver Charles Jarrot stole the legs of a table at his hotel to replace his Napier's damaged wooden frame. And there are many tales of the terrifying mountain section: how the drivers had to lash their feet to the pedals to prevent their being thrown out of their seats on to the rough roads; how they only just managed to negotiate the dizzy drops; how the vitals were torn away from the undersides of the cars as they hit deep drainage gullies straddling the road.

Cars fought duels at 80 mph through clouds of dust that rendered everything over six feet away totally invisible. Corners were taken flat out under these conditions: the drivers kept a navigational eye on the tops of telegraph poles to judge the position of approaching bends. Some drivers even raced the express trains running on a railway line parallel to part of the course.

Selwyn Edge in his 40 hp Napier won the Gordon Bennett Trophy, a shorter event to Innsbruck, run within the Paris-Vienna race. But the greatest and most unexpected victory was scored by a small Renault driven by Marcel Renault himself. The car was no more than a quarter of the size of the main contenders, but Marcel managed to drive it over this nightmare course so fast that he arrived at the finishing line in Vienna before the officials were ready to receive the winner.

The first Grand Prix

By 1903 capital-to-capital racing on public roads had become too dangerous, so the French staged a Grand Prix race (the term was borrowed from the horse-racing world) at Le Mans, in the Sarthe region of France.

In 1906 the first of the now traditional Grand Prix motor races was held over a two-day period during the hottest June for years. Once again a Renault scooped the prize for France, with Hungarian driver Ferenc Szisz at the wheel. A Fiat driven by Nazzaro was just behind him.

About this time some engineer-designers had begun to look askance at the way cars were becoming larger and larger, with engines up to a gargantuan 18 litres. They designed cars with smaller, more efficient engines, and in 1906, the same year as the first Grand Prix, they raced them. This, the first organised light-car racing, eventually put an end to the giants of the earlier years. Small cars like the tiny 1.3 litre Bugatti proved that science, rather than sheer bulk, paid off.

In 1912 a young designer presented a new car at the Grand Prix grid — a Peugeot with an overhead camshaft engine: a car that with *pilote* George Boillot at the wheel, became a world-beater — until one day in 1914 . . .

Everyone knew the French Grand Prix was going to be a duel between Boillot's Peugeot with its four-wheel brakes (then new to racing), and the 4.5 litre Mercedes team, carrying only rear-wheel anchors. The relative braking power at corners could easily make the difference between victory or defeat. The race was won by the clever tactics of the German team, who deliberately instructed one of their drivers to set a too-fast pace in his Mercedes, hoping to goad the excitable French ace into an indiscretion. The ruse worked. The German guessed that Boillot would not allow anyone to pass. Boillot was the French favourite.

One of the most dramatic motor races is the Monaco Grand Prix, fought out around the streets of the Mediterranean principality, past shops and cafés, under bridges and along the waterfront. This is an early advertisement announcing the 1930 Grand Prix.

The Fiat company of Turin, Italy, were strongly represented in motor sport in the first decade of the century. This later two-seater racing version of the modest 1.4 litre Fiat 501 also won several important events, including the 1922 Targa Florio, a gruelling race around Sicily.

Bugatti, the jewel of all racing and sporting machines of the 1920s. Finely-made and precisely engineered by the 'Maestro' Ettore Bugatti at Molsheim in Alsace-Lorraine, France, fewer than 10,000 cars were built in a production spanning 30 years. This Bugatti is a 1926 car of 2261 cc, supercharged.

A 1936 supercharged ERA. This was the British challenge in the light racing field, and the English Racing Automobile Company, led by racing driver Raymond Mays, scored many victories.

This was a French race. He *had* to lead the field. Sailer in the 'decoy' Mercedes speeded up. So did Boillot. At 90 mph in places, they hurtled round the circuit. Finally Sailer's engine cracked up and he retired from the race. Boillot was triumphant, and the French crowd went wild.

But the Peugeot, too, was mortally stricken by this chase, and soon Boillot ground to a creaking halt, while young Christian Lautenschlager of the Mercedes team cruised past to win. The race taught motor sport enthusiasts many lessons and was one of the first examples of team tactics — a stratagem that has been used many times since that breathtaking event in 1914.

Central to the sport of motor racing were the rules governing, or restricting, the size of the engines, the weight of the cars, or sometimes the distance they could travel on a set measure of fuel. There were many disagreements between the sporting authorities, the designers, the drivers and the manufacturers, all of whom had their own points of view. The engine-size regulations — the 'formula' for the top-class racing cars — changed every few years during the 1920s and 1930s. The old 4.5 litre formula was dropped quickly after the first world war, and the 3 litre engine maximum brought new cars to the circuits — and

Still often regarded as the most powerful racing car ever built, this 1937 Mercedes-Benz W125 had an amazing 646 hp available from its 5.7 litre engine.

also brought, in 1921, the first big American victory on the track in Europe.

The race was once again the French Grand Prix — and the hero of the hour was Californian Jimmy Murphy, who drove his Duesenberg to a dramatic win against the best Europe could put on to the grid. His 78.22 mph victory proved that four-wheel brakes (they were the first hydraulic brakes to be used in Grand Prix competition) were by now essential for racing. Today hydraulics are used in virtually all road vehicles; just one example of the way in which lessons learned on the racing circuit are passed on to ordinary road users.

When in 1922 the racing formula was cut down to 2 litres, the size of many family car engines (although aero-engine development had introduced eight-cylinder units into regular use), the Italian Alfa Romeo and the French-made Bugatti became the top rivals for the great prizes of the circuit.

The great endurance race

It was in the mid-1920s, too, that other types of motor racing took shape. The family man was beginning to look around for a car, and he wanted to see some speed contests involving the sort of cars he might be able to buy for himself. Thus the great endurance race, *Les Vingt-Quatre Heures du Mans* (the Twenty-four Hours of Le Mans) was born.

The first of this famous round-the-clock series was flagged off at 4 pm on 26 May 1923. It was a day and night marathon, with drivers changing place every two hours. The cars were 'practical touring cars' with full road equipment.

Le Mans was a terrific success with the public and the racing world alike. At first French cars won; then the colourful Bentley victories brought fame to the sports-car maker from London. Alfa Romeo took over in the thirties, sharing the honours with Bugatti; and once, in 1935, a British Lagonda was given the winner's chequered flag. The fifties saw no less than five superb victories for Jaguar; and the sixties were a constant battle between the red Italian Ferrari and the Anglo-American Ford GT40. Later marques such as Porsche, Matra and Renault have also won Le Mans, the world's most colourful motor race.

The revised formula of 1934 brought about great changes in Grand Prix motor racing. The so-called '750 Formula' demanded only that a car should not weigh more than 750 kilogrammes, and said nothing at all about engine size. The result? Two German firms built cars that were light but strongly constructed, and that housed enormously powerful engines. One of them is still the most powerful racing car ever made.

The marques were Mercedes and Auto Union; the first known for its high quality cars; the second a combination of firms (Audi, Horch, DKW, Wanderer) formed in 1932. Before the thirties were halfway through the accolades of motoring racing belonged almost exclusively to them.

The first racing Auto Union appeared in 1934, a car designed by Dr Ferdinand Porsche. New world speed records immediately hit the news headlines. The rear-engined car — the first to be successful in racing — won almost everything in 1936. Daimler-Benz had also shown the first of their Mercedes Silver Arrows, the cars that were to become legendary, and which appeared again in modern form twenty years later to win again all the world's major prizes.

Then in September 1939 the human tragedy happened again. Peacetime sports came to a halt while another war razed much of Europe . . .

By the early fifties motor sport had been re-established, with new cars and new heroes. 'Newcomer S. Moss,' as he had been called earlier by the press, was by now the great Stirling Moss; his rival, the legendary Argentinian Juan Manuel Fangio (*El Chueco*, 'Bow-legs,' to his friends). The new World Championship title was the main goal of the top drivers, and cars like Maserati, Ferrari and Gordini (and by 1954 the second generation of Mercedes-Benz), battled for the chequered flag on the circuits of Europe, and later in Africa, America and the Antipodes. Fangio, perhaps the world's best-ever racing driver, captured the World Championship no less than five times before retiring in 1955.

The sixties saw smaller cars, rear-engined once again, with Jack Brabham and others from countries 'down under' capturing the world titles. A run of home-based British pilots also took the title: Mike Hawthorn in 1958; Graham Hill in 1962 and 1968; Jim Clark 1963, 1965; John Surtees 1964; Jackie Stewart in 1969.

What of today's sport? Rallies, Formula racing, grand touring, saloon and sports-car racing, hill climbs, speed trials, sprints, kart racing, drag races, autocross, rally-cross and so on, provide sport all the year round. And the Grand Prix calendar is crammed with Formula One contests for most of the year. Today's cars — the turbo-charged Renaults, the Lotus, Williams, Ferraris (oldest marque in the sport), Maclarens, Arrows, and others — still compete on the circuits at ever-increasing speeds (up to almost 200 mph on some of the straights) in the tradition of those rugged heroes of the first Grand Prix back in 1906.

Until recently, most of the cars used the engine that has been popular for several years — the Ford Cosworth V8 3 litre unit. This and turbo engines are now close rivals. The drivers, no longer mostly British as they were a couple of decades ago, are from France, South America, Italy and Germany.

Today, some eighty years after the first Grand Prix held on that rough circuit at Le Mans, Grand Prix racing is still healthy — and still represents the ultimate in motor sport.

Grand Prix racing, 1982. A dramatic shot of the Grand Prix Renault RE 308 Turbo V6 piloted by Alain Prost.

World Champion at Brands Hatch. New Zealander Denny Hulme won the Championship title in 1967. Here he drives a Formula 1 McLaren.

One of the toughest of modern rallies is the East African Safari, a high speed contest over roads that may be washed away by rain or blocked by wild animals! Here a Peugeot splashes through a mud-covered track.

. . . and a rally for the oldies. Every year two or three hundred cars built before 1905 take to the London-Brighton road for a gentle spin down to the coast. This 1903 Renault is crossing South London.

The business end of the Formula 1 Alfa Romeo V12 during a 1982 Grand Prix, with de Cesaris at the wheel.

SMALL WORLD

The magic of miniatures, either toys or models, fascinates children and adults alike, and the world of table-top transport has captured the imagination of many since it all started a hundred years ago.

Toys and models have been made for our delight since model-making enthusiasts saw the first, crude, full-size cars rattling out of their cobbled stableyards, and we have been well supplied with treasures for the toy cupboard throughout the history of motoring.

The earliest were usually tinplate models, operated by wind-up clockwork motors. Others were pull-along or push-around models, and were often made of wood. Pedal cars (with cycle-type crank and sprocket) were made during the early days of motoring, and Edwardian examples are now collectors' items.

Cast metal cars, buses, trucks and so on were made later, and eventually took over from tinplate as they were safer to handle. Today plastics of various kinds are used, as well as accurately-moulded cast metals.

A tinplate toy from Germany made in about 1906, called 'Uncle and the Naughty Boy'. When wound up the boy tries to steer, receiving a sharp tap from uncle's cane.

Lehmann was one of Germany's early tinplate toy makers. Many manufacturers came from Nuremberg, the old clock-making town in Germany. The London double-decker bus was a favourite with all of them.

Another beautiful Edwardian toy, this phaeton has finely-made lamps and a starting handle.

The famous Paris bus in tinplate miniature. About 35 cm long this is now a sought-after collector's piece.

For the boy with everything. This sit-in scale model of a Bugatti Type 52 racer has pneumatic tyres, padded seat, hand brake — and an electric motor operated by the driver.

Meccano motor-car constructor's set for the budding engineer of fifty years ago. A clockwork motor, rubber tyres, wheels, two types of body, radiator, and a choice of body panels enabled the youngster of 1935 to build his own dream car.

Treasures of the thirties; an open tourer passes a London taxi. Made by Triang, both taxi and tourer are pressed steel, and the car's uncomfortable passengers are die-cast lead.

More a model than a toy, this cast example of the famous world land speed record-holder Golden Arrow is an accurate copy of the real Irving Napier now in Britain's National Motor Museum at Beaulieu. In 1929 Sir Henry Segrave created a new world record of 231.44 mph in Golden Arrow.

WORLD ON WHEELS

'Buy one for each foot!' said the wits in the press. 'Small and cuddlesome,' enthused others. Some laughed; some ridiculed the tiny car and called it a toy. But Herbert Austin just smiled at their jibes. He knew he had built a winner.

The year was 1922, and the first post-war spending spree had run down. The public still wanted wheels, but they had to be cheap and simple to run. So Austin designed an 'infant prodigy', sketching out the first rough plan on his billiard table at home one night. The little car was a faithful replica of a full-size four seater vehicle. Just 8ft 8ins long, with a pocket-sized 747 cc engine, it had room for two adults in front and two children in the back seat.

The new Austin Seven was exactly what the young family needed. It handled like a real motor car, could do fifty miles to the gallon, and cost, by 1923, just £165—a price that undercut most motor-cycle-and-sidecar combinations just enough to swing buyers away from the open-to-the-weather world of bikes.

By 1927 the Austin Seven was being made under licence in Germany as the Dixi, in France as the Rosengart, and in Wilmington USA as the Bantam. In Japan an imitation Seven was made by Datsun. Herbert Austin's billiard-table baby had acquired world fame.

Several other motor manufacturers were producing small cars too: Citroën of France introduced a little 5CV (5 hp) in 1922; and Italy's Fiat began to mass-produce the 501 (they were keen on numbers instead of names), a 1.5 litre in a choice of matchbox-shaped saloon or open two-seater.

Germany was to make—and sell in large numbers—its own 'small man's car' a little later. The oddly-named Opel Laubfrosch (Tree-toad) first rolled off the line at Russelsheim near Frankfurt in 1924. It, too, had everything a big car could boast: a side valve four-cylinder engine; pressure lubrication; electric self-starter; inside gear lever; disc clutch. It could scamper along at up to 45 mph and developed 12 hp. The cars were all painted a froggy green colour.

Other countries were making 'basic cars' at this time, and Britain was in the fray with several more examples. One, the Morris, was a main contender for top sales, while a dozen other small manufacturers up and down the British Isles were producing cars made from bought-in parts, as rapidly as eager buyers could drive them out of the showrooms.

Great manufacturing energies were spent in satisfying the needs of the mass market in those golden 1920s. The days of motoring as a luxury only for the rich were over. However luxury cars were still being made in large numbers during the twenties and thirties. The French-built Hispano-Suiza started a modern trend with its overhead camshaft unit, at a time when many important manufacturers still used old-fashioned side-valve engines. Fiat and compatriot Lancia made V-12 cars. Napier, Guy,

An early post World War I product. This French Benjamin cycle-car with its tiny 5 hp engine was an attempt to manufacture a modest car for the thousands of young men returning from the armed services with a little cash in their pockets.

'Buy one for each foot,' they joked when the Austin Seven first appeared. But the little 747 cc engine gave 13 bhp — and that meant it was a real car, not just a 'four-wheel motor-cycle' like some of its competitors.

Opel of Germany made this very popular little 'Laubfrosch' (called Tree-toad because of its rather reptilian green paint) in 1924. It was almost a copy of the Citroën 5CV and caused some legal trouble before it became the first real German 'people's car'.

George Lanchester was Britain's first genuine car manufacturer. This 1919 Lanchester 40 hp saloon was one of his most elaborate models, with finely curved panels and domed roof. This car was laid-up for twenty-four years, during which time it was painstakingly kept clean (and examined after early wartime air-raids) and is still in fine condition.

Another modest British car of the early 20s. The 9 hp two-seater Belsize Bradshaw was unusual in that the engine was oil-cooled and much less noisy than most others of that date.

The two great German firms of Daimler and Benz amalgamated in 1926 to become Daimler-Benz; their cars were then called Mercedes-Benz. This is the sober and solid eight-cylinder Nürburg of 1928, in a dramatic travel poster.

The hardest wearing of them all, the Austin Twelve, introduced in 1921. It was one of Herbert Austin's most successful designs, even though overshadowed by its smaller stablemate, the Seven. The car was produced as a taxicab as late as the 1940s, so durable was its design. This is a 1928 1.9 litre Clifton tourer.

Rolls-Royce and Bentley with their reliable six and eight-cylinder engines (Guy had the eight) were distinguished names in Britain. In France Gabriel Voisin produced cars that looked like aeroplanes drawn by Picasso; and other thoroughbreds like Delage and Bugatti also caught the public eye. Germany began making some impressive Mercedes sedans, and later went on to build some of the most startling and powerful sports-cars the world had ever seen in the Mercedes-Benz K, SK, and SSK.

Into the thirties

The motor industry began to change in the thirties. Gone were most of the lightweight cycle-car makers, the mushroom firms of the past, the backyard 'assembled' car makers. They vanished overnight as the world depression of the early thirties forced small companies to close down.

Manufacturing techniques were changing too. Early cars had been carefully made in two major parts. The engine and running-gear were the province of the engineer, and the body the work of the old traditional coachbuilder. Car buyers would purchase their model—an Austin 60 hp, a Rolls-Royce Silver Ghost, a Thorneycroft 20—in chassis form, then order the body to be made and fitted, often in a style that was unique. Now with every family man hoping to own a motor-car, methods had to be speeded up and costs reduced.

Alvis Speed Twenty, 1932. This British sports-car of open-road days was one of the most handsome vehicles of its day. It is now a coveted collector's item.

Vauxhall sporting line. This, the impressive 20/60 hp Hurlingham of 1931, was produced by the Luton company after joining forces with General Motors. It had a boat-tail, dual cowls, a big 3317 cc engine — and was the last of the pioneer Vauxhall sports-cars in the 30/98 mould.

Britain has a large number of motor museums, ranging from the National Motor Museum at Beaulieu, Hampshire, to small private collections that are open to interested visitors. This is Doune, in Scotland, which has a small but unique collection.

Pressed-steel body frames were used for most cars of the thirties, with the exception of the 'grand luxe' models. And with under-powered engines suitable only for quiet family cruising, the run-of-the-mill saloon car often became a rather dull vehicle. However, with so many new motorists on the road, most of whom had no experience at all, cars with only a little surplus power were thought to be safer. Not that this mattered a jot to their owners. The open roads of Europe and America (America was building new roads at last) were beckoning—and there was great fun to be had out there!

Motoring conditions were indeed almost idyllic. Motorists driving the same make of car considered themselves to be in a sort of users' club, and would salute each other on the road when passing; and of course would always stop to offer help if they saw another motorist in difficulties. Miles of open road without another vehicle in sight, experienced only in remote France or deepest Wales today, were common, and driving was a thrill for the adventurous. Open cars, with their pipe-smoking drivers wrapped in flying scarves, would cruise happily for miles at 40 mph. Only occasionally was there a slower car to overtake, and there was rarely anything coming the other way. And of course the AA or RAC scout was there to salute the proud motorist if his member's badge was in evidence on the radiator of his vehicle.

The open road

There were three distinct classes of motor-cars in the thirties: the tinies—which meant the Austin Sevens, the three-wheeler Morgan runabouts, and the 500cc Fiats. Then there were the family cars for Sunday runs and holidays while the children were growing up: Singers, Citroëns, Opels, Standards, Morrises and so on. And there were the quality carriages: Bentleys, Daimlers, 'Grand Turismo' Alfa Romeos, the distinguished Graf und Stift limousines from Vienna. Germany still supplied the motoring world

with large, dignified Mercedes-Benz saloons and sports vehicles (the two original companies of Karl Benz and Gottlieb Daimler had joined forces in 1926), and the Bayerische Motoren Werke (BMW) was moving slowly into the quality car world.

The legendary Hispano-Suiza, a car that conjured up the mood of the twenties, was still being produced. During World War I the French factory had made large aero-engines, and when peace returned the technology developed during the war was used to produce a superb model—the H6B, a 6.5 litre 100 hp luxury car with finely

Developed from the Aston Martin team cars that won their class at Le Mans in 1931, this 1934 Aston Martin Le Mans Mark II sports two-seater is a rare post-vintage thoroughbred.

Mercedes-Benz economy car, 1934. The whole motoring world was making economy cars then, and this 150H (H for Hintern, meaning rear-engined) had a small four-cylinder engine of 55 bhp.

engineered mechanics and servo-assisted four-wheel brakes, something few other large cars boasted in 1919. This was perhaps the only vehicle that ever really challenged the Rolls-Royce as top-of-the-tree in the motor world during the twenties and thirties. However, what the British Rolls-Royce lacked in advanced engineering, it more than made up for in its complete reliability, its silence and comfort, and its imperial architecture. Every successful man wanted one, and Rolls-Royce had built a factory in the USA in 1920 to satisfy a clamouring American market.

There were plenty of competitors in the USA also clamouring for a place in the quality end of the market during the thirties. The Pierce Arrow, an auto for the connoisseur if there ever was one, was one of the three most aristocratic of American automobiles (the Three Ps—Packard, Peerless and Pierce Arrow). Starting in 1901 at Buffalo, NY, the marque carved a niche in American history as high-grade transportation, a 'head of state' car and later a film star's town carriage.

America's big motor companies, some of them new corporations, had risen to the height of their wealth and power

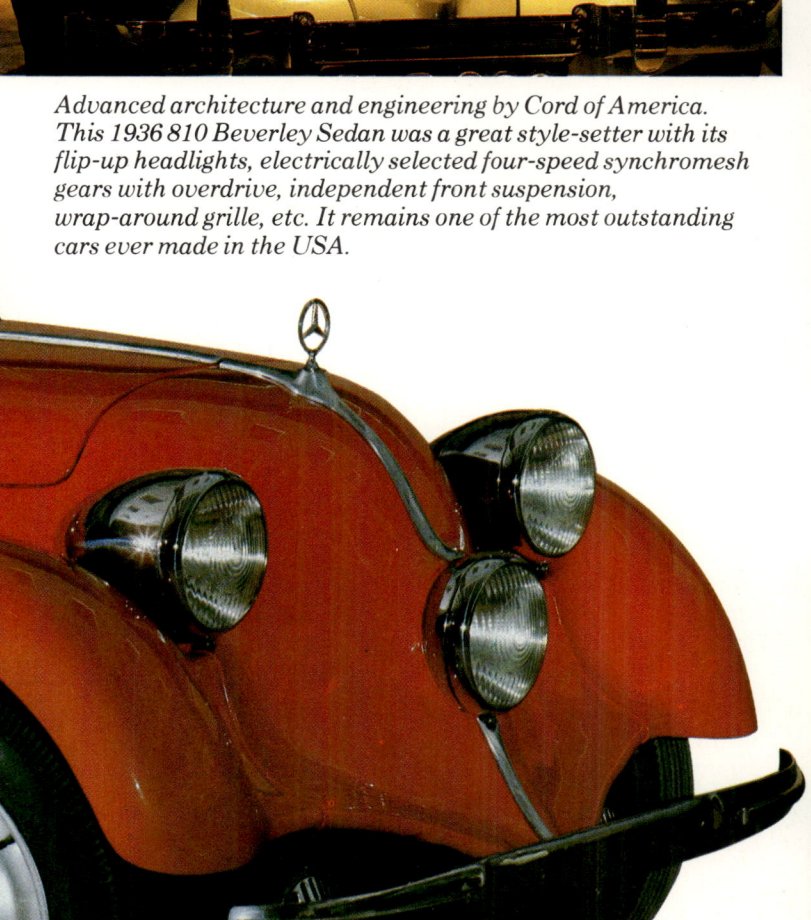

Advanced architecture and engineering by Cord of America. This 1936 810 Beverley Sedan was a great style-setter with its flip-up headlights, electrically selected four-speed synchromesh gears with overdrive, independent front suspension, wrap-around grille, etc. It remains one of the most outstanding cars ever made in the USA.

'First in luxury and first in prestige' runs the advertisement in an American magazine for the Cadillac Fleetwood of 1937, offering V-engines in eight or twelve cylinders, or enormous 7.4 litre sixteen-cylinder units giving nearly 200 bhp.

The 'Japanese' look of the fifties caused most American cars to present a large grin to oncoming traffic. The 1953 Buick Skylark was a fiftieth anniversary model. For the first time eight-cylinder engines proved more popular than six-cylinder units.

The other contender for the title of the finest piece of automotive engineering from the United States must be the Duesenberg SJ, made in Indianapolis. Maximum speed was 129 mph, and acceleration from 0-100 mph was just seventeen seconds. Nothing else on American roads could out-perform it . . .

Opposite above: One of the great cars to come from the Stuttgart company, the Grosser Mercedes-Benz 770, a superb six-cylinder 7.7 litre engine developing 150 bhp (200 with a supercharger.) This model was much in favour with the higher-ranking officers of Germany's Nazi party.

by the late thirties. The Ford car was part of a way of life, seen in every street in all parts of the globe. General Motors, still a giant concern today, produced cars under the banners of Cadillac, Buick, Pontiac, Oldsmobile and Chevrolet, and had bought up other companies in Britain, Australia and Germany. GM's claim was that they made one car in every three produced anywhere in the world.

The third motor empire in the USA was Chrysler. Former railwayman Walter Chrysler had made his first car in 1923, and by the thirties owned a complex that included Dodge, De Soto and Plymouth. A few brief years later Chrysler put his factories to use making war materials, helping in no small way to win the largest war the world had seen. Some 25,000 tanks left Chrysler's factory gates, nearly half a million army trucks, and a host of other military machines during the 1940s.

The thirties were days of progress in several aspects.

The cars of the period were easier to drive than those of the previous decade, which was a blessing for all those new learner drivers who could never have mastered some of the terrors of 'crash' gears and double-declutching. They were cheaper, and so were available to the less wealthy buyer. They were no doubt safer, if only for their inability to 'scorch' along. On the other side of the coin, the decade brought, with the increasing number of motorists, the beginning of the modern malaise—the traffic jam, pollution of the air, motoring accident casualties...

However, the thirties were the years of the open road; still open enough for driving to be a pleasure, with traffic jams only in the largest cities. For the first time the ordinary family man could hope and plan for his own transport, saving enough to buy a modest vehicle for perhaps £150. The car changed from being a luxury item, as in the early days, to become a useful machine for both work and leisure.

At the 'mini' end of the size-and-price scale in the 1930s was this
delightful little Fiat Tipo 500 Topolino, 'Little Mouse.'
With a diminutive 570 cc engine it could take two
people over the mountain ranges of Italy with
reliability, if not in great comfort.

A CAR IS BORN

Since Ransom Olds 'invented', and Henry Ford developed, the system of mass-production before World War I, car-making technology has progressed dramatically. These days, with electronic machinery and robots, a factory may be operated by a handful of white-coated technicians seated at control consoles. The cars, complete and ready for road testing, are turned out at the end of the final assembly line almost untouched by human hand! However, human expertise is still needed at some stages of the complicated business of designing and getting a new model on to four wheels and into the showroom.

The first decisions are made at management level: 'What sort of car shall we produce? Should it be a standard family car? Should it be front-wheel drive? Should it have a new engine, or an improved version of the current one?' Then the designers get down to work and plan the car itself, first in general terms, then in a three-dimensional scale model and in technical detail. Preliminary work on the design may be done as much as eight years before we, the public, see the finished 'production' car in the showroom.

Testing hand-built prototype models is followed by a 'pilot build'—when perhaps a dozen cars are made using the tools and plant that will make the actual production car for the first customers.

Later, the press are invited to inspect and drive a first batch of up to 200 examples, which will have been weeded out for 'rogues'. Meanwhile the first consignments of production models are sent out to the motor dealers, ready for the great day when the glossy new vehicles are shown to the customers.

1. Some manufacturers start at the beginning... smelting ore to make the basic material for the car — pig iron.

2. Austin Metro sub-assembles being welded on one of the factory's four welder lines at Longbridge.

3. Fiat automation. Here Fiat Strada bodies are being made, each stage of the car moving from point to point to be welded or assembled entirely by electrically-controlled and programmed machines.

4. A Metro 'automatic body framing' line, also completely automated, with fourteen robots carrying out the body-frame welding and assembling.

5. A cathode dip tank. Here the primer is applied to body surfaces and body sections, using electro-painting methods.

6. Completed body shells sail overhead, waiting for the next stage in assembly at the Volkswagen Golf plant.

7. Fitting the floor trim on a Golf assembly line Wolfsburg, Germany.

8. After final assembly Golf cars queue up to be driven off the end of the production line . . .

9. . . . for a final check of engine, brakes, running gear and so on.

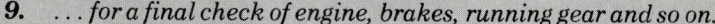

THE BEST OF TODAY

What has been the most exciting modern development in the automotive world? Was it the appearance of the Citroën ID in the fifties, years ahead of its time with its bold new design? Was it Britain's Mini, launched in 1959 and eagerly bought by a public who needed a small car to use in ever-more-crowded cities? Was it a technical advance — disc brakes for example, a new and more efficient way of stopping? Perhaps it is the safety aspects of today's car — the rigid passenger box and crumplable front and rear sections? Or is your imagination captured by one of the most dramatic cars ever made, the E-Type Jaguar, still the favourite of film stars, sportive drivers and model-makers?

The cornucopia of motoring goodies that has poured from designing boards and factory assembly lines over the past thirty-odd years has been aimed at every market, ranging from cars that cost more than a family house to those that cost little more than a motor-cycle. The Lilliputian Citroën 2CV, 'four wheels under an umbrella', was for people with no money to spend on luxuries. The Fiat 600 type of 'basic' cars, now offered by several nations, was designed for the young person who desperately wanted something better than a rain-soaked journey to work on a moped . . . And so on up the scale to the Lamborghinis, the Mercedes 500 SLs, the Aston Martin Lagondas . . .

The 2CV was a classic example of the ingenuity of designers who had to work within strict limits of cost. It was first sold in 1947, although it was originally designed

The sleek and low Jaguar XJS. With a 5343 cc V-12 engine and 150 mph at its command this is the stuff of dreams…

before World War II. The French 'minimum' car, as it was called, was exactly the right vehicle for car-hungry buyers of the 1940s. It carried four people; it had no frills, no expensive gadgets; it used very little petrol in days when motor fuel was still rationed; and it was cheap. The 375 cc flat twin-engined car was started by a handle (a pull-string starter had been tried out earlier!), had simple mechanics — and just one headlamp. But it could travel 65 miles to the gallon at speeds of up to 40 mph.

At about the same time, a factory in Germany was struggling back into production. It had been bombed badly during the war, and its plant and building wrecked. The name of the company was Volkswagenwerk. Dr Ferdinand Porsche had designed a small 'people's car' under Hitler's instructions, and had tested the first models by 1936. Then the war came and the car — for which many Germans had already paid a cash deposit without ever having seen one — was switched to a wartime role and produced as the Kubelwagen (bucket car), a light jeep-type car. Later an amphibian car was made. Called the Schwimmwagen, this military VW could be used on road, field and reasonably calm water.

Wolfsburg, home of the Volkswagen, was in the British Occupation Zone after the war and the first batch of about 1500 civilian 'beetles', made painfully and slowly with what was left of the factory, were used by the British forces. The Volkswagen beetle's shape hardly changed at all over the thirty-odd years of its European production. By 1961 VW were selling a million a year, and by 1972 over 15 million of them had been made, passing the legendary

Ford Model T sales record of nearly half a century earlier to become the world's best-selling automobile.

The biggest boost to British motoring morale in the gloomy postwar years must have been the Jaguar XK120, a sleek and glamorous two-seater performance car that first appeared at London's Motor Show in 1948. Almost as soon as it was introduced it started to win sporting prizes: the Tourist Trophy; the terrifying Coupes des Alpes Rally; and countless racing circuit victories. The powerful 3.4 litre engine with its twin overhead camshafts proved so successful that today it is regarded as a classic design. This car, too, quickly became a world's bestseller in its class, a worthy descendant of the prewar SS sports-car line. But the XK120 was only the beginning: the Coventry company had further plans.

It was the E-type that gave the second Jaguar jolt to the motoring world. In 1961 an ultra-fast sports-car, which looked like something between a racing car and a missile, appeared. Derived from the racing C-and D-types, it had all the thrill of fast travel and all the built-in stability necessary for fast handling. This was a car that could match the sporting Mercedes and Aston Martin — and made their high price look a little ridiculous. By 1974 the E-type had acquired a V12 engine of over 5 litres, and was beginning to bow out to its successor — yet another Jaguar 'fantastic', the fixed-head sports coupé, XJS. . .

Mini miracle

It was dubbed 'The magnificent Mini' as soon as it appeared in late 1959 — here was another car for a motoring world that was getting more crowded.

Small was the plan for the Mini: a plan that was so successful that the little car looked bigger inside than out! Its transverse engine, front-wheel drive and rubber cone all-independent suspension, and of course its compact size, were the result of some brilliant original thinking by designer Alec Issigonis, who had already designed the

Aston Martin DB2/4 MK III 2+2 coupé. A complicated title which means that this classic car has a powerful engine designed by Bentley: room for 2 in the front, but is a tight squeeze for 2 in the back.

Like its big brother the Grand Prix Renault, the Renault 5 Turbo uses the turbo engine and has a 112 mph top speed. The model is aimed at the young businessman who needs a small car for town travel, but with a turn of speed and élan. The picture shows an experimental model.

Postwar pioneer, a 1950 Triumph Renown. Introduced in 1946, the car's styling broke new ground with its 'knife-edge' contours and its large windowed rear. It still has the look of an aristocrat.

France's postwar baby was the Citroen 2CV, the car that was described as an umbrella on wheels. First shown in 1948, its flat-twin engine-buzz can still be heard all over France. This is a 1951 model.

best-selling Morris Minor some years earlier. The first prototype Minor was, he thought, too tall and too narrow. So he had the car cut in half along its length, and a ten-inch section inserted down the middle, giving the Minor a wider, more road-hugging appearance.

The Mini (Issigonis brought the new word into the English language) was an immediate success, although it had a few mechanical problems at first. It was entered in races and rallies, and became a household name overnight. Young people took to the Mini in a big way: it was cheap, small, manoeuvrable, and a lot safer than many imagined. It was also the springboard for other vehicles: the Moke, the larger-engined and GT versions; the super-tuned racing Minis; and Rileys and Wolseleys that were really Minis with more knobs and chrome.

The small car trend set by Issigonis sparked off a generation of similar 'Minis'. The motoring world was rapidly becoming nose-to-tail and the pioneering British car had solved one of the most pressing problems of the day — how to get a quart into a pint pot! At ten feet long, the Mini was just half the length of some of the larger American cars — and four could fit sideways (perhaps a little uncomfortably) in a US regulation parking bay.

Second generation 'superminis' blossomed all over Europe in the late 1960s and early 1970s: the Fiat 127; the Peugeot 104; the Renault 5. And today we also have the Japanese family: the Dihatsu Charade; Datsun's Cherry and others.

Here we must mention Ford: Ford, the world's greatest pioneer motor maker; Ford, the man and the company that first put the working world on wheels. The Ford V8

The greatest invention since the wheel.

Mini

First seen in late 1959 the British Mini, with its 'sideways' engine and compact design started a worldwide trend to smaller cars.

The Mercedes-Benz 230SL of 1963, with its distinctive Pagoda roof. It later grew into the 280SL, and so on up to 500SL. This is the 450SL, an eight-cylinder 4.5 litre car of very sportive character.

Chrysler Newport 1979. One of the most distinguished marques in the American motor world. The Chrysler corporation includes Dodge and Plymouth, and the cars named after Walter Chrysler himself.

'A cross between a missile and a racing car', said a British motor magazine of the Jaguar E-Type in 1961. The early ones housed a 3.8 litre engine of classic design and sported a bonnet that some thought looked like a duck-billed platypus!

The Dodge brothers John and Horace set up business in Detroit, first building engines for Ford. When in 1914 they made their own first car, they started to build a company that in the twenties rose to second place in overall US car sales. Chrysler bought the company in 1928 for $175 million. This is the smart Dodge Omni.

The Renault 14L, the first Renault to house a transverse engine, used a Peugeot unit. Volvo, Renault and Peugeot worked together to produce the best engine.

Pilot was the first car to be seen in Britain after the gap created by World War II, followed by the Anglia, another 'minimum' car with no frills behind its old-fashioned but hard-working 1172 cc engine. The public bought the Anglia and its partner, the Prefect, eagerly in those postwar days, and buyers had to promise to keep their new car for at least two years before selling it — for it could be resold next day for at least twice its official price to a car-hungry public.

Ford milestones mark the years of motoring. The Thunderbird appeared in 1955. America's motor sports fans went wild. Here at last was a true US sports-car from Ford, the first the company had made, and a challenge to the only other American sports-car, the Chevrolet Corvette. The Mustang followed in 1964: this was a 'pony' car for the young buyer, and could be fitted with either a modest 3.3 litre engine, or others up to large V8 units. By the end of the first year of its life, Ford had sold no less than 400,000 Mustangs.

Back in Britain the best-seller Cortina was launched in 1963, followed by the 2+2 Capri coupé which was a little like a scaled-down Mustang. It too, was a low, sleek model with a turn of speed, and in 2.8 litre form could clock up 120 mph. Then the Fiesta, another Ford winner in the small car range. Not quite a Mini, it was designed for space-saving, and has an east-west engine with front-wheel drive. Lastly the new-style Escort was born in 1979, and the Sierra in 1982. Made in twenty-seven different variations, today's Sierra can be all things to all owners — from the basic 1.3 litre version right up to the very powerful 2.3 litre Ghia, which has a top speed of 110 mph, and all the engineering of high class sports machinery.

Britain's latest favourite, the Vauxhall Cavalier. This is the 1.5 GL hatchback model, a four-cylinder, 90 hp car that feels and runs like a six-cylinder car.

The long-life Ferrari. This is the 308 GTBL of 1982, a 3 litre low profile 'bolide' with a touch of magic about its shape — and its 150 mph performance.

Honda Prelude from Japan, popular size, popular shape — and with a choice of opening the window or switching on the air-conditioner.

The enduring Porsche 911 was first seen in 1964, since when the Stuttgart company has added a dozen other numbered models to its range. But the 911, the classic Porsche shape, still remains on the new car lists in at least five different forms, from the 'bread and butter' 911SC to the exotic Turbo.

Porsche magic

Porsche — a name that conjures up the image of magnificent sporting vehicles; of countless victories in gruelling rallies in Europe or Africa; of swift travel along Germany's sweeping autobahns — is still at the top of the performance car list.

Surprisingly the Porsche had quite a modest beginning. Dr Ferdinand Porsche, who had designed the Beetle Volkswagen for Hitler's Germany, based his first prototype Porsche car on the Volkswagen, using a simple platform frame and an air-cooled engine at the back. The first Porsche was in fact just a neatly-designed Volkswagen sports-car.

Ferry Porsche, the designer's son, was responsible for the first small production run of the little Porsche 356, an open-to-the-wind, rear-engined, hand-panelled vehicle with just 40 hp in its one-and-a-bit litre engine. But it went like a real sports-car, its highly-tuned power unit giving 80 mph with rocket-like acceleration.

The Porsche five-cars-a-month programme escalated rapidly, and by 1951 the Stuttgart factory had rolled out its five hundredth car.

When in 1964 the new Porsche model was unveiled it was to be called the 901. However that number was 'booked' for another company, so Porsche called it the 911.

That magic number is now the hallmark of the finest in the sports-car world. If you could see the pride with which the Porsche bench workers at Stuttgart stamp with a metal die their own initials into 'their' engine block when their work is complete, you would understand why the Porsche reputation is second to none.

Porsche have added several more numbers to their line: the 912, 914, 924, 944, 928 racing sports-cars of the 1960s; the 904, 906, 908, 910, 907 and so on; and the 4.5 litre 917 which started life with a dramatic win at Le Mans in 1970, the first of its many victories on the circuits of the world.

Meanwhile the 911 continues to be improved. The 911 Turbo is perhaps the most famous of them all today. First seen in 1974, its 3 litre turbo-charged engine made it the fastest accelerating production car in the world. And its almost magnetic roadholding qualities are such that very few drivers ever get to its 'unstick' point — and those brave men that do find that even then the Porsche is a near-perfect blend of powerful sports vehicle and safe-handling deluxe coupé.

A Rolls-Royce Silver Spirit, still top of the tree in 1983; still luxuriously dignified, with its classical 'Parthenon' radiator; and still with an immensely powerful performance at the driver's fingertips.

INDEX

(italic figures denote illustrations)